The Gifts the Ocean Gave Me

Lauren da Silva

Starfish Stories Publishing

E-Book ISBN: 978-1-990419-42-3

Print ISBN: 978-1-990419-43-0

1st Edition

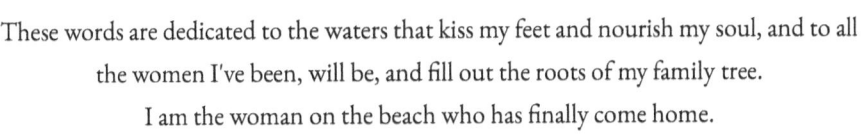

These words are dedicated to the waters that kiss my feet and nourish my soul, and to all the women I've been, will be, and fill out the roots of my family tree.

I am the woman on the beach who has finally come home.

table of contents

descent

shield

I am descended
from a long line of eldest daughters,
each one inheriting a world
that is laid on her shoulders.
the entire weight
of the whole lives of
their husbands and fathers.
her children, sisters, brothers,
and eventually, their mothers.
together with the cursed shield
forged from the fury
brewing inside their bellies,
the only nourishment
for this family tree
is a surge of feminine rage,
and the shame.
the shame that these worlds are, in fact,
too heavy for our bruised backs to bear.
I tried to burn it down once,
under the peach tree back in waco...
but I have been bred for my broad shoulders.

my daughters will ask about them one day
and I will tell them
that atlas is a woman,
and that they have permission
to let the whole world down.

how?

how can I love
someone
who taught me
how to
hate myself
so well?

belittling

there is only
one thing
more painful
than having
an accomplishment
belittled.
and that
is having it
ignored.

you, my dear
are a master
of both.

being

how is it
that I must
somehow,
not only
forgive my self
for its humanity?
but you,
I must also
forgive you
for teaching me
that my humanness
is also
my shame.

baggage

when I stop,
I unravel.
when I cry,
I cry alone.
chaos
has been my comforter
and peace
a threat to that cocoon.
I became the very best helper
who was unable to help her.
a malnourished
survivor, starving,
& perfectly,
unlovable too.
my needs,
forever negotiated.
yours,
an oath
I have died to keep.

died, without
ever knowing
how to even begin
living.

cptsd

I used to think
that I was
'just angry'.
but apparently,
anger
is just
anxiety's
other name.
and that anxiety
is another way of saying,
'chronically dysregulated'
and that being chronically dysregulated,
is another way
the body likes to say,
"I'm hungry".

I must be starving.

I wonder?

I wonder,
has anyone
ever
looked over at me
in wonder?
has my joy
ever
washed over them
and become
theirs?
or has my delight,
have I,
always
been so triggering?

an insurmountable threat
to their own
misery.

journey

I was
never lost,
never *really*
alone.
just wandering.
but
not alone,
not once.
my map
was made up
of stories
they made up.
my compass,
calibrated only
for relief,
reprieve.
if I could just
get far away
enough
from myself...
then maybe,
I could outrun
the bleeding,
the screaming.
I would be
far away enough
from the whimpering
and the cries.

I've wandered too far
by wandering away.

but I've never gone far enough
to find my own (way).

my turn

"you have to leave,
because it's *my* turn,
with her...
my time".
freudian slip.
slip of the tongue.
slippery words.
slippery like my mind
and the places
it takes me
when I'm slipping.
slippery like my steps
when my knees are weak
from being held onto
with nothing to hold onto.
needed for everything,
and needing everything, too.
"it's *my* turn"
to need.
to hold.
to take.
to eat.

you have needs that
you'd like me to meet,
but do you even know them by name?

dissonance

I know
very well
which version of me
you prefer
and which parts
you resent.
the pieces of me
that disgust you,
because
they must remind you
of all the ways
you disgust yourself.
does the mirror flinch
when *you* flinch
at your own reflection?
does it recoil
in shame
the way we both do
when you look over at me?

is she capable
of remembering
that it's not her
you hate,
but what
you see in her
that looks
just like you?

spontaneous combustion

our house is
burning down,
but how
can we save it,
when
every tear
I cry
just starts
another fire?

grief

grief is a galaxy,
dark and cold,
beautiful,
and strange.
vast.
there are black holes
that scream with agony.
pockets of light,
in an endless night.
I am told
it is my job
to 'hold space'.
to remain open
to the feeling,
to *simply* hold
space.
?
(an entire galaxy
is a lot
of space
to have to hold.)
is the work of grief
to stretch myself
until I can
wrap myself
around it,
like God can?
(does he?)
or
is it to float
in-between

the planets, moons,

constellations & rocks?

to surrender

to whatever winds

can blow in a vacuum?

what if

I erupted?

would my tears

become the stars?

does grief

eventually

make you a nebula?

would you call

it beautiful then?

from your backyard porch

with your wine,

pointing

in wonder,

at the balls of burning gas

dripping

from the origins

of my ache.

when I can finally

look up,

would I be able

to live with it,

to love it, then?

procrastination

sometimes (most times),
I fool myself into thinking
that knowing a lot about something
(anything really),
is a suitable substitute
for actually doing something
(anything really),
with what I know.

what a shame,
such an extraordinary
amount of time and effort.
what an obesity of knowing
in an otherwise
malnourished life.

chosen

For as long as I can remember, I have been waiting for some grand romantic gesture. I've been waiting for my mother to choose me, for my father to choose me. As a teen, I started to hope for a boy to recognize what was right in front of him all along, to notice the priceless treasure everyone had overlooked, and choose me.

I grew up, got saved, and got married, and somehow, I am still waiting.

Waiting to be more important than the trauma or the pain.
To matter more than a career,
or a girlfriend,
or a business deal,
or another girl,
or his boss,
or his parents.

Waiting for a grand declaration of love that would in some way, shape, or form finally declare my value.

Appraise me.

I would be chosen and because someone else would acknowledge my value, I would be finally worth something. I could finally feel worthy.

Except, what if I would always be waiting? Rationally speaking, I know it is absolutely ridiculous, and yet here I am. If they won't notice, maybe I can show them?

Maybe, If I were beautiful, thin, and amicable enough, they'd choose me.

Maybe, if I accomplished enough: got the best grades, earned the title, all the titles, if I gave more of myself away than she did, and expected even less than she did in return... Maybe then they'd finally see what a good deal I was.

If I attended church enough, read enough books, did enough 'work', if I scrubbed or hid or boarded up enough of my unsightly bits... would I be 'unbroken' enough?

Would they love, care for, and tend to me then?

If I traveled far away enough? Crossed enough oceans, gave enough of myself away...if it was convenient enough for you, if you didn't even have to get up off our couch, or put down your phone, would I have gone far enough for you?

Only if it is also true that I am yours to give, push, scrub, and polish away.

But I am not.

What if I am not yours to appraise or to value? Or to not value? What if I am not yours to accept or reject?

What if I belong to me?

What if I am mine?

What if I have been mine all along?

It all belongs to me.
I belong to me.
I am mine.

I have been waiting for *me*.

I am waiting for *me* to stand outside of my window with a bouquet and a boombox. I am waiting for *me* to notice and see what's been right in front of *me* all along.

I am waiting for *me* to choose me.

In big grand romantic gestures
and small, steady & consistent choices.

I am *mine*.
I belong to *me*.
I can choose *me*.

Even if it was July.
Even if it is August.

Even if it was the 999th of November
Or way down in February
I choose me.
Every time.

I choose me over and over again
because that is how it should be.

I choose me.

awakening

pruning

the farmer arrives
with shovels,
leather gloves,
ploughs.
tools and protection.
friends, old & new,
uninvited guests.
lives intertwined.
I cling to them.
hugging their necks in protest.
stay!
and suffocate me,
I don't know how to breathe
when I am not competing for air.
familiar tendrils are torn away,
as I pass out parting favors,
pieces of myself,
souvenirs of my hospitality.
remember me, please?

at the end of the day,
there is space
and there is pain.
disorientating
room to grow.
nourishment in plenty,
because I'm finally eating alone.

protection

maybe my perfectionistic, fault-seeking,
chronic, brokenness-repairing frenzy
isn't the dysfunctional part I thought it was.
maybe it's the shield
that protects me from the
vulnerability I experience
when everything is enough
and I am deeply satisfied
with me,
and you,
and them.
and life is actually pretty good,
and it all feels,
I feel
too good to be true.
that the other shoe
might just drop.
and if I settle into this goodness
just a little too much,
get a little too comfortable
with all this joy,
and if I start to build a home in its warmth,
that it would eventually,
inevitably,
all burn down.
and so,
I erect the shield
that picks every nit,
fixates on every fault,
and hoses down
every ember

...because nestling into joy
is a dangerous way to be
in a world
that likes to play with fire.

the table

at church, they told me not to build walls or lock the doors,
but to make room and build bigger tables.
I was told to love all of my enemies.
unless of course, the enemy was me.
'host everyone
except yourself.
banish her,
dissect, mutilate, and dismember
her.'
only room for the proverbial,
metaphorical stranger
but not the parts of me
that were too strange.
everyone held the deeds to my love,
except for me.
no.
I needed washing,
cleansing,
isolation,
purification,
exile.
perhaps the house they had me build
was just a trap
and the table,
surgical.
lured in with a warm meal
and a place to stay,
but no place to just be.

the big secret
is that if you're using the table
you're building

to tear yourself apart
then the house you're building
isn't a home.

it's an asylum.

breadcrumbs

you can tell how small a family/partner/culture/system

wants you to stay

by how little nourishment

they throw your way.

breadcrumbs,

if you're lucky

of support, validation, appreciation, affirmation,

and love.

'how could she expect even a milliliter more than a drop?', they mutter

while praising the inches that peel from your waist.

'doesn't she know it's her birthright to give?', they'll gasp

and whisper behind cupped hands

as you become a shadow, starving.

or worse still,

have the audacity to walk away.

...when you find (or build) a new table

and feast on praises, appreciation,

reciprocity and safe, boundaried love.

when you have the impertinence to get fat

and take up actual space in your own life.

when you learn to live so fully that you actually feel full,

satiated.

"who the fuck does she think she is?"

they'll murmur.

while you smile,

facing the sea,

well-fed,

and feasting on your own bounty.

humus

'body and soul', the 'bible' said.
body - untrustworthy, dark, and dirty.
soul - destitute, but with enough work, saveable (from itself).
they told me we weren't evangelicals
but how else would you explain our fear of humus?
our humanness?

they told me Jesus was fully human
and then spent decades trying to convince me not to be.
saving me from the earth,
the soil, and womb that made me,
the only cradle that's ever truly nourished me.

growth

I woke up today
with the distinct feeling
that my whole life was falling apart.
and instead of
scrolling,
eating,
drinking,
reading,
numbing.
I cried.
I reached for the paint.
I went for a walk.
and I wrote a poem.

I woke up today with the distinct feeling that my life was falling apart
and
that I was also coming back together again.

permission Slip

where can I get a permission slip
for this 'terrible' day?
a day where the dog got out, twice.
the children got hurt,
and your best friend left.
a day where the sun shone softly, graciously
and you painted, then designed a book cover,
took a nap, and wrote a poem.
for days when you are full.
of regrets,
shame,
and an obscene amount of caffeine.

armchair

what makes a moment well spent?

when there's a poem?

a painting?

a revelation?

a meal?

a prayer?

a dollar

to show for it?

or

is my being in it,

enough?

my presence,

am I

enough?

if all I "did" was

breathe

and stay

with my breath,

with the blood bathing every cell,

with the oxygen washing into each one,

with the carbon dioxide as it made its way out,

with the lymph moving on,

with every electrical impulse,

with life itself.

is a moment a waste,

when all it did

was hold space

for me?

sovereignty

I can hear her before I see her.
the low hum of overthrow in the distance.
an avalanche is on her way.
I can feel her before I see her.
the surge rising in every single cell.
a tsunami on the horizon.

she arrives:
rain beating down on my cheeks.
winds swirling in my chest.
my rage finally makes landfall.
"welcome back, loyal friend".
"I've been waiting for you".
I bunker down, and wait it out.
listen in the darkness
as she goes to work,
laying waste to the ways
I have been standing aside,
abandoning my agency.
she decimates what I have built in self-betrayal.
purges the places & platforms that I used to give away my own power.
castles of compromise lie gutted by her truth.

at dawn:
as her winds go from howl to whisper
I emerge in sunlit silence
to survey the destruction
to meet who she left behind.
waiting patiently in the aftermath
smiling softly.
"welcome home, sovereignty."

apprenticeship

intimacy

if our silence digs the canyon,
truth builds the bridge.

solar systems

are we *really* all suns?

or are we just planets vying for our moment in it?

are each of us *really* our own universe,

each one with all of our own glory,

burning at its center?

if we are the sun,

then who are our planets?

who serves who?

the sun, sharing its warmth and light?

the planets orbiting around her?

clamoring for proximity...

turning their faces toward her in gratitude...

unbridled adoration.

if I were the sun,

would I still need the shade?

night?

water?

winter?

if I were the sun,

would my toes tickle the space where the ocean licks the shore?

would my fingers caress the wild grasses as they hug my waist?

would my chest rest under the soft hum of a sleeping cat?

would I need to set myself on fire to shine?

would I need to stand alone, yet surrounded.

suspended at the center,

disconnected,

too dangerous to touch?

would I light a thousand horizons,

visible,

vital,

distant?

if I am an entire universe...
sun, moon, stars, planets, darkness & light
do I need to build one to prove it?

resilience

my whole life
the world has been teaching me
to be constantly
increasing
my capacity
for stress, pain, and difficulty.
it has been coaching me
in the art of dissociation
from myself
and you.
stay busy.
work hard.
give it all away.
keep scrolling.
do it all.
don't stop.
'you're making the world a better place'
by your selfless self-erosion.

an intolerance for suffering
has never been my *real* problem.
as a child
the doctors applauded
my unusually high
tolerance for pain,
even on the day
it nearly took my life.

what if
what I need
to be truly resilient
is more peace

more joy
more love
more connection,
and more sensitivity?

what would the world
be like
if I had learned
the art of
being big enough
to hold more love?

decisions

we lay in the dark,

stars glowing above,

ocean roaring on my left,

babies breath to my right.

gophers and their tunnels below.

gophers and their deep, dark, penetrating tunnels,

burrowing into my back.

fear burrowing into my brain.

we've pitched our tent

and the gophers have their tunnels.

the sand has its soft, shifting temperament,

it's uncertainty.

what if we're swallowed whole?

all of us consumed,

swallowed by the sand,

lost inside the gophers' maze.

"but if you know how

to build your nest", whispered Heron.

in the tallest pines,

kissing the sky.

reed by reed,

woven carefully.

reed by reed,

swaying, but up high.

gophers go low,

& herons need the sky.

reed by reed,

I'll weave our nest.

swaying,

dancing in the wind's gentle whispers

swaying.
and sturdy.

hospitality

one thing I know about this life
is that, in order to remain open to the beauty
you must also remain open to the pain.
you must live with your heart unguarded,
like a door always unlocked.
always ready to welcome the next ecstasy,
or the next crushing defeat.
you don't get to choose your visitors,
or the gifts that they bring.
sometimes,
they'll hold healing
and suffering inside the same hand.
to take hold of the one,
you must also receive the other.

all you can do is welcome
and receive each one openly enough,
and be courageous enough
to receive the next.
never lock the door
and to never turn life away
when she knocks.

bad mood

I used to think that all this "work"
(this personal growth stuff)
was about never having to suffer the indignity
of letting shit get to you again.
that it was about no more bad days
or bad moods.
it was about being so impenetrable
that one day,
once I'd done enough "work",
I'd have changed 'enough',
be good enough,
to build and maintain
a life perfect enough
to be pain-free.
and when I was
perfect & perfectly inoculated,
 I'd finally be able to say,
"I love you"
and mean it.

now I know
that the work
was never about bending my curves into straight lines,
or about beating any part of me into submission.
it was never even supposed to be "work".
it was about learning to be safe enough in my own hands
to be soft again.
it was about learning to love the edges.
smooth, curved *and* jagged.
accepting and lovingly holding their "not-straight-lined-enoughness".
staying tender with them on bad days
and during bad moods.

making them tea,

tucking them in,

and letting them rest.

reminding them that they're more

than the sum of their bent and broken bits.

the work

(and remember, it's not *really* work - it's gentler than that)

is about getting through bad moods,

and bad days,

and hurting hearts

without heaping on the shame

or band-aiding with blame

it's about loving them just the way they are,

however they arrived that day.

much like you were always meant to be.

to be able to say, "I love you,

you are enough,

and good,

...just the way you are."

and mean it.

beauty

some moments aren't meant to be captured,
or frozen in glass
on a screen,
or in time.
they exist only for your enjoyment,
for right now.
for savoring,
the way you do a fine chocolate
as it melts slowly, delicately
within the warmth of your mouth,
wrapping itself dreamily around your tongue.
one of the most important things you can learn,
is just to let it be,
and to just be with it.

some moments weren't born
to be taken captive on your screen.

joy

joy is a prayer, too.
God doesn't delight in your misery.

dreams

my dreams take me back
to old houses,
down old paths
with old people.
like they're one last chance
to walk through the house.

-one last time-

to check under each bed,
to scan the sides of each road,
to search each eye.
to take back anything
once left behind,
belongings long forgotten,
recover the treasures buried,
abandon the hatchets.

-one last time-

before we lock the doors,
hand over the keys,
and set sail for new lands.

dreams aren't always prophecies,
sometimes,
they're eulogies, too.

'broken'

I have spent way too much time
thinking about the shells
littered along the shore
of my favorite beach.
or rather,
their pieces.
broken bodies
scattered,
like ashes.
crushed,
ground up by the sea's fury.
passed over by the shellers
and tourists.
too broken,
too incomplete.
at sunrise, they sparkle,
broken bodies dancing
in the water
and the sunlight
that destroyed them.
are they *washed up*?
or are they just,
washed up?
after a lifetime of swaying through
the waves, tossed about,
surrendering in the currents.
what have they seen?
where have they gone?
whose soft bodies have they housed?
how they've lived!
and now,
they rest

in pieces,

and in peace.

used up by their lives,

at rest in the sun,

on the sand:

living my bucket list life.

blessed even,

to escape the buckets,

glass jars,

and sticky fingers.

a gentle end

to a violent death,

and a glorious life.

squeeze

I used to try to fit every single dirty dish I had
into the dishwasher at once.
trying to stay on top of things.
desperate to stay ahead.
but you can't stay on top of dishes
or get ahead of them
unless you've also stopped eating.
isn't that what kitchens are made for?
the messy business of nourishing a life?
you can't stay on top
of a sumptuous, nourishing life
or get ahead of it.
you can only stay inside of it.
you can live hovering around or above
but never participating in
the dirt, the joy, the love, the grief.
dishes won't ever stop coming
and you will always need to eat.
now, I leave pots in the sink
and glasses on the counter,
and I lick my fingers,
when I bake cakes.

peel your potatoes slowly.
let the earth get under your fingernails.
there will always be another load.

safety

do you *really* save
the life of a candle
by leaving it
to the solitude
of the shelf or
the darkness of your desk drawer?
suffocating
safely
and alone,
waiting for the special occasion
to shine?

wouldn't *you* rather go,
with your hair on fire?
ablaze in your own glory
and purpose
until you're nothing
but a wisp of smoke,
a pool of wax
and an entire lifetime of light?

the (w)hole

sweetheart,
to become who you are
you also
need to come to terms
with your softness.
you must become comfortable
with the discomfort
of simply being alive.
alive,
not just,
as in not-dead
a-live (*uh*-**lahyv**),
a life...
a live (liv) - as in
actually-living.
the salty, sandy spray
from the ocean's mouth
is supposed to sting.
death
is supposed to be excruciating.
loss
is supposed to leave a gaping hole.
and you,
you are supposed to leave it there.
learn to touch it gently
with your bare fingers
and caress the spaces
where love once lived.
but don't stuff it,
it is not a starving mouth.
stay soft,
and live tenderly.

leave room for longing.
remember the places
where your love
once lived.

leave your flowers
in the doorways, at the tombs,
and on the grave.
face the salty, stinging, sandy spray
and weep.
and then,
keep living.

wild orchids

orchids are *actually* air plants.
outdoor.
air. plants.
plants that flourish,
(it turns out)
naturally,
in the wild
air.
all this time
I've been told
they're *too* sensitive
too troublesome
too difficult to keep alive.
all this time
I've left them indoors,
staked,
and in pots.
safe
and contained.
all this time,
they've preferred
the wilderness.
freedom for their roots,
and stems, and leaves,
and blooms
to roam.
to be wherever
and however,
and whatever the fuck they want.
all this time,
they didn't actually mind
the wind,

the rain,

the sun,

or change.

all this time

they've been pretty,

pretty resilient.

hardy even.

in the wild.

maybe,

all this time

I have not

been *too* sensitive,

too much work,

too troublesome,

or *too* difficult to please.

Just contained.

maybe,

all this time

I'd have been more at home

in the fresher air,

where the sun can color

and speckle my cheeks

whenever and however it likes.

where the wind is free

to run its fingers through my hair,

where my heart & soul can roam wild.

where my roots

and blooms

can just be

whatever,

whoever

and however the fuck

they want to be.

the angry tirade of a wellness bro at the beach on a windy day

how dare it be wild?
and unpredictable?
inconsistent?
and inconvenient?
'I paid two whole dollars for my hour!'
but now there's water
and wind
and sand
-everywhere -
the waves have taken over the entire beach.
what a pity.
I used to like to work out
right. here.
and now,
now it's high tide,
and it's changing.
it's different
in winter!
and it's cold and windy!
in the winter!
I've always preferred it in the spring.

too dangerous?
when has she ever been safe?
there have always been sea monsters
lurking
beneath the surface
of the summer.

the dance

the moon isn't just reflected light
she's also energy.
tremendous.
not the sun.
but just look at what she is capable of when she dances with the sea...
together these shifts preserve, cleanse, and nourish life.
how dare we insist on their stagnation?
I came here suffocating in the arms of shame
baring my 'inconsistencies',
my ebbs and flows like a mill stone around my neck.

as the wind wipes my tears,
the moon
& the sea whisper:
fluctuating is our honor,
a privilege,
& our purpose.

holy ground

she's spitting mad,
but is still kissing the shore.
foaming at the mouth,
and the foam is velvet.
she's churning,
but it churns crystal,
blue, and turquoise.
it's unsafe,
but it's clean.

we all remove our shoes
and while some curse the tempest,
others join the dance.

aftermath

thirty-six

it *is* a gift,
I tell myself,
to age.
to grow older,
'maturing',
I tell myself
as I awake to 36,
applying lipstick to ever crinklier lips,
following lines across my face,
across the map,
along the ways I've been,
the roads, canyons, and wastelands
I've navigated to be here.
it is a gift.

*my life
is a gift.*

enough

the kids watched a lot of tv this afternoon
and I berated myself.

and now:
they're dancing in the dusk-lit glow
of the kitchen
while I cook dinner.
we're laughing,
and they're twirling,
and we're together.

and maybe,
just maybe
this isn't just 'enough'...

it's everything.

priorities

I am sure there are a million places
I could be
and even more things
I should be doing.
but for now,
I am barefoot
in the afternoon sun
on a pool chair
under a palm tree
with a sopping-wet five-year-old
lying against my chest.
mary oliver rests in my hand
and florida's wintery fingers
comb through my hair.

actually,
I am quite certain
I have nothing to do
today,
other than this.

iphone photography

a photo.
a photo of a dog.
a big dog.
a big, smelly dog.
a big, smelly dog shedding,
laying on a blanket.
a big, smelly dog shedding
all over a blanket reserved for guests
on the floor.

"momma! thank you for picturing this! I love him."

women on the beach

I love how when women are at the sea,
we breathe
and bathe deeply,
and leave replenished
and full.

not because we're finally on holiday,
but because we've all finally made it home.

love

I *really* love that I
am learning to
fall in love my life.

have you ever?

have you ever felt the late afternoon sun
settle itself over your body
like a blanket
as the late afternoon breeze twirls
it's fingers through your hair
in whisps and whispers,
as you lay in the lap of the earth
on her bed of grasses, or clover
before they've ripened crimson, or white
for the bees?

have you ever been held by your humanity
long enough to know
that it is the light,
the air,
the earth,
and the water,
in and around you
that makes you so.

that time i saved the cat from the great blue heron

I kiss the ground
as she bellows
at the cat
that I just scooped up
from her feet

the sound of it,
up close...
I have the audacity
to look her in the eye...

and weep.

sorry, not sorry

I am sorry,
but I don't want to
show you everything
there is to see.
just as the ocean keeps her secrets,
I'll guard mine.
if you want to know her
you'll have to sit alongside
and wade in.
and after days, months, or even years
you will still not know it all.
hold your breath for as long as you can,
your deepest breath would not be deep enough,
still.
sit alongside me,
on the banks of my soul.
I'll show you parts,
and you can know me in pieces.

I am not sorry.
I don't think you should hold your breath for me.
some parts are too deep
for shallow souls to see.

homecoming

beautiful body,
tender soul.
home is in the fresh morning mist.
barefoot in the soil, or the sand.
being kissed tenderly by the sun.

winter swim

twinkling dusk,
lightly afloat.
shimmering heart-songs
with delicate dances.
twirling around
in the darkening blue.

onlookers

oh what a gift
it must be
to not even see
the eyes
peering over
or through
the hole in the secret garden wall.
in curiosity?
or is it mockery?
jealousy, more likely.
to not even look
at the onlookers.
to not lend them your eyes
or a small corner your mind,
or even a second of your time:
the only key to this magical world
you've created
just for you.
and for me.
what a gift
it is to get
to see,
to bear witness to
and not be seen.
to be a guest,
to not intrude
on the magic
that is your childhood.

magic spells

mama, you're the sun.

xx

mama, I love your smell.

xx

mama, your eyes are like flowers.

church

the gulls who seem to enjoy donut holes.
the sandpipers,
even that one with only one leg.
the young brown pelicans,
and the white ones.
the turtles, are brand new
and have been returning for millennia.
the shells, old mollusk bodies, fractured, in their millions.
every grain of sand in my hair,
down my pants,
and on my feet.
the pompano shoals
and the sea ducks.
the early risers
and the sunbathers.
the locals
and the holidaymakers.
the seagrasses
and the moon jellies.
the portuguese men of war,
on the beach, and in the surf.
the tides, the depths, the shallow pools.
the sun
and the clouds that rain on her parade.
the wind and the swaying palms,
those who dance in reverence to it all.

this is church,
and we are one another's holy ground.

perfection

I awoke
this morning
to dim, quiet light
and soft, robust aromas.
sweet, shallow breaths.
deep purrs.
quiet and gentle droplets.
my love.
my life.

xx

is there any thing quite as lovely
as a cozy spot
with hot tea
in the gentle winter rain,
nestled peacefully
in the liminal space
sometime between the solstice
and the spring?

xx

if there is a time and place for productivity
surely this is not it?
unless movies and books and hot tea
and hair braiding and afternoon naps and
hot baths are in fact,
productive?

xx

I do hope
that I can be happy

and full here.

I *do* feel full in solitude,

guiltily so.

like it's some forbidden and indulgent pleasure.

it might be because I was left alone a lot as a child,

or because people have always taken a bit too much,

or perhaps as Ron says, because that's

just who I am:

completely satisfied, absolutely satiated, and full

alone.

when I am old

inspired by 'warning' by Jenny Joseph

when I am old
I will make quilts that I'll turn into coats
and hats
and they won't match.

I'll live as an old crone in a cottage
by the sea
with my cats,
and my flower garden,
and my sea chickens.

I'll bathe naked in the sea,
in the moonlight,
and I'll be the one standing guard
as the grandmothers,
the great leatherbacks,
and the loggerheads
return to shore to build their nests.

I'll be the one watching over
their babies as they erupt from their sandy wombs
and make their way to their mothers
and the ancient sea.

I'll stay up all night
and howl
at the full moon with my friends.
I'll wait on the shore for the sunrise,
kissing the surf with my toes.

I'll drink wine, and eat cake, and bread
spread thick with butter
and french cheeses.
the shape and comforting softness
of my body will please me.

I'll regularly admire my freckles
and praise the lines on my face,
the silver in my hair.
will be my reward,
and I'll call myself beautiful.

I'll paint,
turn a pottery wheel,
interpret dreams,
take naps in the middle of the day,
and make love.

I'll make up for the sobriety of my youth
and its shameful innocence.
I'll be devilish,
unapologetic,
and proud.

children will love me
and I will enjoy them.

In the meantime,
I'll practice
being too little for some,
and too much for others.

I'll become just right for me:
bolder, colorful,
and more and more
spacious each day.

this, just in case
I wake up one day,
from my youth
and gasp,
turning in fright from
the me I discover in the mirror.

I might be strange,
but I won't be a stranger
to myself.
when I am old.
I'll be shameless:
a wonder.

epilogue

observations I've made after spending a year at the feet of the sea:

The Ocean: I never know what version of her I'll get, and yet, I always find her to be absolutely beautiful. I appreciate all of it and I long to be appreciated in the same way. The ocean doesn't ask for anyone's permission to be what, or how, or who she is at any given moment. She just is.

Perhaps she just knows she is *that* glorious. I have noticed that people tend to find rip currents, a shark, or dangerous surf inconvenient, but I don't think she gives a shit. Does *anyone* have the audacity to believe she should just always be open for business? Available to the purposes of the masses on demand? She is so big, so beautiful, so powerful, and so mysterious that only a fool would dare to, and they'll live their whole lives disappointed in and frustrated by her.

I'd like to permit myself to just be an ocean. I too, am moved by the moon in ways that I don't understand, or even dare to control (at least, not anymore). What if that entire phenomenon is actually more like a dance? Why am I embarrassed, ashamed, or frustrated that I get to participate in such a glorious mystery? I, too, am deep. I too, contain multitudes. She is my sister and my mother, and I want to come home. I want to *be* home.

Notice that it is only a particular kind of shore-dweller that gripes about what she *appears* to be on the surface. When have you ever heard of an ancient Loggerhead griping? Or a Great Blue Whale? The Great White? Not even a sardine or hermit crab would be foolish enough to complain - they know her depths best of all and are even thankful for them. They appreciate her nourishment. It's the humans, of the taking kind who think she should be more predictable, and tame. Perhaps it is the same with my own (takers, that is).

"Stay close to those who know and love your wild, child. Those who appreciate your depths, who know they are nourished by them, but also nourish you in return. Choose the ones who stand in awe at your dance with the moon, and who delight in what happens to you in the wind.

For anyone who wants a domesticated sea, doesn't really want the sea - only its treasures."

about the book

The poems in this collection tell the story of a woman recovering from the chaos of her life and of this world. It is an account of her finding herself and loving herself. It is a journey of discovering and a proclamation: "I am enough for myself and that is enough. It is everything." – *Mandi Barnard, early reader & beloved friend.*

about the author

Lauren da Silva is a South African writer, poet, publisher, and artist living in Boynton Beach, Florida. Her work explores and celebrates the beauty & wisdom found all around us in nature and unearths it from the deepest and truest parts of ourselves.

Lauren started drawing, painting, and writing as a young girl but parted ways with her creative side and its gifts as she got older, and started to get the impression that there were more important things she ought to be doing, and more valuable contributions she ought to be making with her life. She went on to work in full-time ministry, qualify and work as a social worker, and start a family.

Only after the COVID-19 pandemic and a third run-in with burnout did she realize that a large and important part of herself had been left behind somewhere, a part of her that made life more joyous, fulfilling, and sustainable. She went on to retrieve it and has been expressing herself with prose, pencils, and paintbrushes ever since.

acknowledgements

Meggan Larson: My best friend, cheerleader, business partner. Thank you for believing in me and my work.

Mandi Barnard, Heather Harbaugh, Kelley Stone: Thank you for being safe and kind and honest and generous enough to be the perfect first readers of these words.

Danny, Kaelah, Noah, Ellie: You made these words possible because my life with you has inspired so many of them. More than that, you empower me to create the time and space required to create, and you celebrate what emerges from those spaces.

starfish stories publishing company

'where the girl who reads all the books becomes the woman who writes them'

Starfish Stories Publishing Company was founded in 2022. Its mission is to create a positive impact through beautiful storytelling by authentic voices, sharing inspiring messages of hope and healing in a world desperate for real connections.

If you have a manuscript you would like us to consider, or if you would like more information about our company, visit www.starfishstoriespublishing.com

www.ingramcontent.com/pod-product-compliance
Lightning Source LLC
Chambersburg PA
CBHW031226120626
46545CB00003B/1019